Melbourne

a panoramic gift book

Steve Parish

Contents

Melbourne

from the heart

Melbourne is Australia's second-largest city, a cosmopolitan metropolis that lives up to its motto: "We gather strength as we grow". In the city centre, gracious nineteenth-century buildings stand beside glass-sheathed commercial towers, symbolising the coexistence of Melbourne's colonial traditions with its vigorous modern lifestyle. Twenty-first-century Melbourne, on the banks of the Yarra River, is one of the great cities of the world.

I spent the first five years of my life in Melbourne and my first contact with nature was along the shores of Port Phillip Bay, so this is a special place for me. I have enjoyed the challenge of capturing its beauty on film.

Steve Parish

The second-tallest residential building in the world — Eureka Tower, at Southbank, looms over other city skyscrapers.

Docklands, on the magnificent Victoria Harbour, is a dynamic combination of residential, retail, commercial and leisure delights.

Inside Melbourne Central, looking up into the glass dome past the giant fob watch.

Simon Rigg's sculptures *The Guardian* ornament the Southbank Promenade on the Yarra River.

A pavement artist puts the finishing touches to a masterwork of public art.

The Big Box Forecourt Exterior at the Melbourne Museum in Carlton Gardens.

Trams ply the broad central carriageway of St Kilda Road, with service roads to either side and the Shrine of Remembrance in the background.

The big men fly – Essendon Bombers play Sydney Swans.

The race that stops Australia – and they're running in the Melbourne Cup.

Docklands, west of the CBD, is evolving into one of the world's greatest urban accomplishments.

The Bolte Bridge, part of Melbourne's Transurban City Link road network.

The Yarra River

Melbourne's mirror

It is nearly 240 kilometres from the Yarra River's source in the Baw Baws to its mouth at Port Melbourne. Along the way, the Yarra waters upland forests and rocky hills, then flows across wide river flats, once tranquil pasture but now increasingly urban.

In the final stages of its journey to Port Phillip Bay, through Melbourne City, the Yarra is bordered by parks, gardens and a multitude of places where people meet to enjoy themselves.

Bridges, carrying all manner of foot and motorised traffic, crisscross it; pleasure boaters, rowers and canoeists cruise its waters; and Melburnians use its banks for picnicking, strolling, cycling, walking and jogging.

A coxless four trains on the Yarra in the early morning.

Solitary scullers penetrate the morning fog blanketing the Yarra.

Non-stop excitement can be found on the Yarra's bank at the Crown Casino and Entertainment Complex, Melbourne's premier entertainment venue.

Southgate

a sensational social precinct

Just across the Yarra River from the city centre is the Southgate Arts and Leisure Precinct, a fascinating complex of shops, galleries, places to eat and sculpture-ornamented riverside spaces. The riverside walkways attract crowds to promenade or watch the street performers. Food from all over the world is available from its international food hall, restaurants and cafés. It is a short walk down the river's verge from Southgate to the Crown Casino and Entertainment Complex, while the theatres of the Victorian Arts Centre are just around the corner in St Kilda Road. A footbridge links Southgate to Flinders Walk and Flinders Street Station, and river cruises depart from Southgate and nearby Princes Walk.

A short walk from the city, perhaps over the Yarra Footbridge (*top*), Southgate is the place to meet, eat, be seen, promenade and be entertained.

A dancing light and water show enthrals passers-by at Southbank.

After Sunset

the city awaits

As dusk falls on Melbourne, the city becomes a place of bright lights and welcoming venues where people gather to talk, eat and enjoy themselves. The city centre offers gourmet delights in areas such as Chinatown, as well as myriad cinemas, theatres, clubs, pubs and bistros. Close by, Southgate, the Arts Centre, Crown Casino and inner suburbs such as St Kilda, Richmond, Carlton and Fitzroy come alive. In the long twilight hours of Daylight Saving Time, Melburnians picnic or barbecue in parks and on the Yarra's banks. Outdoor concerts and theatre performances are always packed, as is any night game of any sport in the city's well-lit stadiums.

Southbank Promenade is enlivened at night by Simon Rigg's two-part sculpture *The Guardians*.

Chinatown in Little Bourke Street.

Melbourne Aquarium on the Yarra's bank near Flinders Walk.

The spire-topped theatres of the Victorian Arts Centre are illuminated at night.

The Eternal Flame burns in front of the
Shrine of Remembrance in Kings Domain.

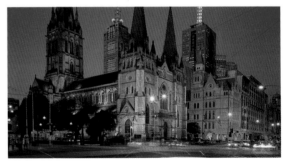

St Paul's Cathedral adorns the corner of
Flinders and Swanston Street.

Melbourne, looking south from the Rialto Observation Deck, sparkles at dusk.

The old terraces in Lygon Street, Carlton, make welcoming restaurants and cafés.

Lights in the trees sparkle along the "Paris end" of Collins Street.

Street performers in Acland Street, St Kilda.

Performing Arts

even the streets are a stage

In Melbourne, the world's greatest actors, musicians and other stars can be appreciated in settings worthy of their talents. The Victorian Arts Centre, just over Princes Bridge from the city, contains a Concert Hall, home of the Melbourne Symphony Orchestra, and a Theatres Building, where productions range from grand opera to puppet plays. For those who enjoy musicals, Her Majesty's, the Regent and the Princess stage big productions, while in the suburbs more intimate theatres play to full houses. Melbourne's International Comedy Festival begins as close as possible to the 1st of April each year, and clubs, pubs, theatre restaurants and the malls and streets feature all manner of performers.

Street performers entertain the crowds of delighted spectators.

Old Melbourne Gaol, built in the mid-19th century, is now a penal museum.

The Princess Theatre, lovingly restored to her present glory and reopened in 1989, stages the grandest of musical theatre.

Heritage

Melbourne's history preserved

Melbourne cherishes its heritage. Although some of its colonial treasures have been lost in the city's development, fine architectural examples have been preserved and restored. The wealth generated by gold mining and rural prosperity funded the building of a fine Victorian city from the 1850s on. The Royal Exhibition Building in Carlton Gardens was the venue for the opening of the first Parliament of the Commonwealth of Australia on the 9th of May, 1901. Buildings such as Como House, the Houses of Parliament, the Windsor Hotel and St Patrick's and St Paul's Cathedrals survive to remind us of the skills of professional people and artisans of the times. Reminders of some of Victoria's most infamous characters and institutions are also preserved, such as the Ned Kelly memorabilia in Old Melbourne Gaol.

Como House, a colonial mansion dating from 1847.

The World-Heritage-listed Royal Exhibition Building in Carlton Gardens.

The grand stairway into the Victorian Parliament House.

The ornate red-brick façade of Melbourne City Baths, dating from 1903.

The *Polly Woodside*, centrepiece of the Maritime Park and Museum.

The Hotel Windsor, built in 1883, is heritage-listed by the National Trust.

An equestrian statue of King Edward VII and delightful floral clock in Queen Victoria Gardens.

Cook's Cottage, dismantled and moved from Yorkshire in 1934, now stands in Fitzroy Gardens as a memorial to Captain James Cook.

Completed in 1910, Flinders Street Station, hub of the city's suburban rail network, is a fine example of the gracious architecture of the late Victorian era.

Light Horsemen on parade, continuing a proud tradition of service.

Shopping

a retail paradise

Most big, modern cities have made a feature of their retail centres, but in Melbourne shopping is an artform. There's an excitement in the air as residents and visitors indulge in "retail therapy" that caters for all budgets. In the inner city are department stores and retail complexes, exclusive boutiques and specialty outlets. The suburbs all have their own distinctive shopping experiences, from comprehensive shopping malls to crowded markets. The Queen Victoria Market has been offering all manner of goods to people from all walks of life for more than 100 years. And after working up a thirst and an appetite, shoppers can refuel their weary bodies at any of a mind-boggling variety of cafés, restaurants or hotels.

The figures of legendary giants, Gog and Magog, have stood guard in the Royal Arcade since 1892.

Chadstone Shopping Centre, where various retail delights await.

In Melbourne, there's a retail outlet for everything...

...sold with enthusiasm and panache by people from everywhere.

Aquarium & Zoo

all creatures great and small

Two of Melbourne's natural history institutions are in easy reach of the city centre. The Melbourne Aquarium mounts fascinating displays of marine life, featuring life on coral reefs, in mangroves and in Port Phillip Bay. There is an Ocean Theatre and a sensational walk-through tunnel that takes visitors into the heart of the sea creatures' habitat.

The Royal Melbourne Zoological Gardens display around 400 species of native and exotic animals in comfortable and stimulating habitats. Exhibits include a breeding colony of gorillas, otters frolicking in their glass-sided pool, Butterfly and Reptile Houses and the Great Flight Aviary.

Underwater wonders on display bring observers closer to another world.

Sharks on display at the Melbourne Aquarium.

The Western Lowland Gorillas at Melbourne Zoo are part of an international breeding program.

The city skyline seen through the masts of boats moored on St Kilda Harbour.

Port Phillip Bay

at Melbourne's heart

The shoreline of Port Phillip Bay is sheltered from much of the turbulence of the open sea, and the Bay's waters abound in marine life. There's magnificent fishing, swimming and boating to be had. The bayside suburbs nearest the city's heart provide watersports, seaside delights and waterside activities that include rollerblading, cycling, walking and jogging. These suburbs also abound in cafés, restaurants, bistros, street entertainments and markets, picnic spots and promenades such as the much-loved St Kilda Pier. As more people seek the tranquillity of bayside living, the urban area has spread right around from the Bellarine to the Mornington Peninsula.

The colourful bathing boxes of Brighton Beach.

Sunrise over Port Phillip Bay.

Dandenongs

a lush, green loveliness

The Dandenong Ranges, only 50 kilometres east of
the city, contain some of Australia's loveliest forest. The
area has been a magnet for city-dwellers for well over a
century. However, today it is still possible to hike along
trails in the Dandenong Ranges National Park without
meeting another soul, awed by magnificent stands of
Mountain Ash, hearing the ventriloquial mimicry of the
Superb Lyrebird resound from the gullies. Dandenongs
villages, with their plant nurseries, galleries and craft
boutiques, are warmly hospitable.

Puffing Billy rounds the bend on its 13-kilometre journey
from Belgrave to Emerald Lake.

The National Rhododendron Gardens at Olinda.

An Eastern Grey Kangaroo and her joey.

Magnificent Mountain Ash forests in the Healesville district.

Healesville

sanctuary for wildlife

Healesville Sanctuary is an ideal place to meet Australia's wildlife at close quarters. The sanctuary is more than just a zoo; it carries out research into wild creatures of many varieties and is committed to breeding endangered species as well as promoting public understanding of native animals and their habitats. Highlights of a Healesville visit are close encounters with Dingos, Common Wombats, Koalas and Platypuses, as well as feeding Australian Pelicans, and spectacular flight exhibits by birds of prey.

A Koala at home in the branches of a gum tree.

Snow fields blanket the Victorian Alps.

High Country

an alpine wonderland

Victoria's spectacular alpine region, popularly known as the High Country, offers great snow sports in winter on the snow-covered, rugged terrain. Two national parks, Alpine and Mt Buller, protect the fragile alpine environment and co-exist with ski resorts, the main ones being Mt Buller, Mt Buffalo, Falls Creek and Mt Hotham. Anglers, bushwalkers and other active people take full advantage of the natural beauty and bounty of the area in spring and summer. During autumn, regional centres, such as Bright, become a blaze of colour as the exotic trees turn gold, red and brown.

Bright's annual Autumn Festival attracts hordes of visitors to admire the autumn foliage.

Phillip Island

penguin paradise

Only 125 kilometres south-east of Melbourne at the entrance to Western Port, lies Phillip Island, joined to the mainland by bridge. Once that bridge is crossed, stress vanishes. The island is famous for its beaches – the rugged southern ones are noted for great surf. Summerland Beach, on the south-west coast, attracts large crowds to its "penguin parade" just after sunset, when flocks of Little Penguins leave the sea to waddle to their nests. Other island wildlife includes Australian Fur-seals, and Koalas, which can be seen up close at the Phillip Island Koala Conservation Centre. Each October the Australian Motorcycle Grand Prix provides thrills for motor-racing fans.

The rugged Phillip Island coastline, viewed from The Nobbies.

A pair of Little Penguins incubating eggs in their Phillip Island nest.

An Australian Fur-seal dives among the kelp at Seal Rocks.

The Great Ocean Road winds along the coast near Lorne.

Scenic Drives

the Great Ocean Road

After World War I, thousands of returned soldiers were employed to build a coastal highway, using picks, shovels and crowbars. The Great Ocean Road was opened in 1932, a magnificent engineering achievement and a memorial to the men who laboured on it.

Today, the renovated Great Ocean Road is one of the world's great scenic coastal drives, linking seaside resorts and giving breathtaking views of spectacular cliffs, islands, limestone stacks, such as the Twelve Apostles, and an ever-changing sea. It also gives access to the green splendours of the temperate rainforests of south-western Victoria.

Erskine Falls in Angahook-Lorne State Park.

Pages 60–61: The Twelve Apostles, off the coast of Port Campbell National Park.

From an early age, Steve Parish has been driven by his undying passion for Australia to photograph every aspect of it, from its wild animals and plants to its many wild places. Then he began to turn his camera on Australians and their ways of life. This body of work forms one of Australia's most diverse photographic libraries. Over the years, these images of Australia have been used in thousands of publications, from cards, calendars and stationery to books – pictorial, reference, guide and children's. Steve has combined his considerable talents as a photographer, writer, poet and public speaker with his acute sense of needs in the marketplace to create a publishing company that today is recognised worldwide.

Steve's primary goal is to turn the world on to nature, and, in pursuit of this lifelong objective, he has published a world-class range of children's books and learning aids. He sees our children as the decision makers of tomorrow and the guardians of our heritage.

Published by Steve Parish Publishing Pty Ltd
PO Box 1058, Archerfield, Queensland 4108 Australia
© copyright Steve Parish Publishing Pty Ltd
ISBN 978174021086 7
10 9 8 7 6 5 4 3

Photography: Steve Parish
Photographic assistance: Ian Roberts pp. 4–5; p. 8 (bottom); p. 9; p. 15; p. 20 (top); p. 21; p. 24 (bottom); pp. 24–25 (main photo); p. 26; p. 32 (top right).
Additional photography: p. 12 (left) Sport The Library; pp. 12–13, Jacki Ames, Sport The Library; p. 29, Tourism Victoria; p. 34, Ian Roberts.
Text: Steve Parish, Pat Slater
Design: Gill Stack, SPP
Editorial: Michele Perry, Karin Cox & Ted Lewis, SPP
Production: Tiffany Johnson & Tina Brewster, SPP

Photo captions: cover, twilight glistens over the city; p. 1, Melbourne city aglow; pp. 2–3, Federation Square; pp. 4–5, Melbourne from the air at dusk; pp. 62–3 Hopetoun Falls, Otway Ranges

Prepress by Colour Chiefs Digital Imaging, Brisbane, Australia

Printed in China by PrintPlus Ltd

Produced in Australia at the Steve Parish Publishing Studios

Steve Parish
PUBLISHING

online

FOR PRODUCTS
www.steveparish.com.au
FOR LIMITED EDITION PRINTS
www.steveparishexhibits.com.au
FOR PHOTOGRAPHY EZINE
www.photographaustralia.com.au